HL

LOOKING AT PAINTINGS

Families

The Guillon-Lethiere Family, 1815
Jean Auguste-Dominique Ingres, French (1780-1867)

LOOKING AT PAINTINGS

Families

Peggy Roalf

Series Editor
Jacques Lowe

Designer
Amy Hill

Belitha Press
London

A
JACQUES LOWE
VISUAL ARTS PROJECTS
BOOK

Text © 1992 by Jacques Lowe Visual Arts Projects Inc.
A Jacques Lowe Visual Arts Projects Book

Printed in Italy

First published in the United States by Hyperion Books for Children

First published in the United Kingdom by
Belitha Press Ltd
31 Newington Green, London N16 9PU

Cataloguing-in-print data available from the British Library

ISBN 1 85561 356 5

Original design concept by Amy Hill
UK editor: Kate Scarborough

Contents

Introduction

*L*OOKING AT PAINTINGS is a series of books about understanding what great artists see when they paint. Painters have been attracted to the subject of family life for more than three thousand years. Some artists have painted loving portraits of their own families. Others have looked at everyday life and special occasions in other homes—from a poor farm in Haiti to a great castle in Spain. By looking at many pictures of families, we see how artists use their talent and imagination to create a personal view of this subject.

Painters are creative explorers. They search their own feelings to show us something about each family group—affection, pride and, sometimes, anger. They often create an unusual mood or a unique setting through the use of colour, **design** and light. With their powers of observation, painters can find something special in everything they see and often invent new painting techniques to express a personal vision.

We will see that Andrea Mantegna created the illusion of soaring space in an ordinary room with a flat ceiling, in *Family and Court of Ludovico III Gonzaga* (page 11). Claude Monet used bold yellow and blue highlights to create the atmosphere of outdoor light around his future wife, Camille, in *Luncheon on the Grass* (page 25). In *Hommage à Louis David* (page 41), Fernand Léger used brilliant colours and industrial forms to express the influence of modern technology on everyday life.

Artists transform what they see into magical images that take on a journey to other times and distant places. You can learn to observe your own family—in everyday activities and on special occasions—and use your imagination to see like a painter.

Note: words in **bold** are explained in the glossary on pages 46–47.

FAMILY SCENE, about 1150 B.C.
Tomb of Inherkhan, Dier el Medineh, Thebes
Unknown Egyptian artist, **water-colour** on plaster (detail)

For wealthy Egyptians in ancient times, life was so good they hoped that life after death would be exactly the same. Their tombs consisted of elaborate rooms covered with wall paintings that were pictorial messages to the gods.

The Egyptian style

Egyptian artists painted figures to show not only what they saw before them but also what they knew was there. The head and the body from the waist to the feet are painted in **profile**, whereas the upper part of the body and the eye are shown straight on. A hand holding an object is usually drawn so that we can see all of the fingers. Egyptian artists, like those in other ancient cultures, drew important people larger than the less important ones. In this painting, the servant is much smaller than the mother and father. She wears no jewellery and is painted entirely in profile.

This unusual way of painting the human figure was essential to the burial ceremony. None of the important parts of the body is hidden, so each figure represents the whole person. Objects were treated in a similar way. A plate of figs is painted as though from above to display each piece of fruit. When the Egyptian's soul awakens, there will be something good to eat. The dead were provided with everything they needed for the next life.

Young children in ancient Egypt did not wear clothes because of the heat, but they had elaborate hairstyles and beautiful jewellery.

FAMILY AND COURT OF LUDOVICO III GONZAGA, 1474
Andrea Mantegna, Italian (1431–1506), **fresco** (detail)

The Marchese Ludovico Gonzaga of Mantua employed Andrea Mantegna to be his official painter. Mantegna painted the Gonzaga palace with frescoes such as this one in which the family awaits the return of the oldest son, Francesco, who had just been made a cardinal of the Roman Catholic church.

Thinking ahead

Andrea Mantegna had to decide in advance how his paintings would look because in fresco the artist paints on to wet plaster, which then dries quickly. First he made a full-size drawing called a **cartoon**. He then transferred the drawing on to the wall and applied a thin layer of fresh plaster only to the area that he could complete in one session. He had to work boldly, quickly and carefully all at the same time. Even with the limitations of

The fireplace is real, but the arched ceiling is an illusion created by Mantegna.

fresco painting, he achieved delicate effects in the individual portraits and in the details of the luxurious clothing.

Mantegna used a painting technique known as ***trompe l'oeil***, which means 'to fool the eye'. The larger-than-life-size figures seem to be stepping out of a small terrace into the palace room. Notice that the marchese's right foot and the hem of the marchesa's dress appear to project beyond the floor of the terrace where they sit.

11

PORTRAIT OF THE EMPEROR MAXIMILIAN I AND HIS FAMILY, 1515

Bernhard Strigel, German (1460–1528), on wood, 71 x 59 cm

By the time Maximilian I became the **Holy Roman Emperor** in 1493, the title had lost most of its importance. He was poor for an emperor, but that did not prevent him from bringing talented painters to his court.

Bernhard Strigel came from a family of successful painters and wood carvers who created religious art for churches, but his special talent was portrait painting. In this picture, Strigel portrays the emperor, his first wife Mary of Burgundy, their eldest son Philip, Philip's two sons, and a grandson. Maximilian **commissioned** this painting to celebrate the double wedding of his grandsons in 1515.

A different style

To please the emperor, Strigel created a highly-finished surface that looks like **enamel**. Among Strigel's other **trademarks** were his use of richly brocaded cloth in the background and an open window with a dream-like imaginary landscape in the distance. The Latin text was added by a later owner who attempted to give this painting religious meaning.

Strigel was one of the first artists to create more casual portraits at a time when most portraits were stiff, and serious pictures of important people from biblical scenes were created for churches. Instead of looking straight out at the viewer, the emperor and his family are talking to each other and show affection. Paintings such as this, which showed the personality and not just the appearance of the sitter, became known as character portraits.

13

RUBENS, HIS WIFE HELENA FOURMENT AND THEIR SON PETER PAUL, about 1639
Peter Paul Rubens, Flemish (1577–1640), **oil** on panel, 201 x156 cm

Peter Paul Rubens had a long and triumphant career creating paintings for many of the kings and queens of Europe. He lived at a time when death at an early age was common. By 1626 he had lost his first wife and three of his five beloved children. Four years later, when he was fifty-three years old, he married Hélèna Fourment and began to raise a second family.

Rubens studied a different pose for Hélèna in this pencil drawing.

A personal picture

Rubens filled this portrait with things that had personal meaning. He chose the elegant Spanish-style clothing to show respect for King Philip IV of Spain, a **patron** for whom Rubens created many masterpieces. The garden design hints at his enjoyment of antiques, and an overflowing fountain represents Rubens' appreciation of Hélèna's youth and beauty. By emphasising Hélèna, Rubens made her gesture and young Peter Paul's response the focus of the picture. While Rubens himself stands back, at the side, gazing lovingly at his wife.

Rubens made the people in his painting come alive through his masterful technique for creating skin tones. He started with a neutral, grey tone and added shadows in the early stages of painting. Rubens then created the flesh tones by applying **transparent** and semi-transparent coloured **glazes** over the neutral paint underneath, allowing the layers to dry in between. As a finishing touch, he painted glowing, **opaque** white highlights.

THE MAIDS OF HONOUR, 1656
Diego Rodríguez de Silva Y Velázquez, Spanish (1599–1660),
oil on **canvas**, 315 x 277 cm

Velázquez was an **apprentice** artist at the age of eleven and a master painter at nineteen. He was an ambitious man who knew that his artistic genius made him equal to the nobles of the Spanish court.

Philip IV became king of Spain when he was eighteen years old in 1621. Two years later, he chose Velázquez to be one of several royal artists. Close in age, they formed a friendship that lasted the rest of Velázquez's life. Philip loved his family and his great art collection, but he was a failure as a king. Spain lost its glory and wealth during his reign and came dangerously close to civil war.

A court official

Velázquez was also the king's chamberlain, the most important position in the palace. His work as a court official robbed time from painting—in his forty year career, Velázquez created fewer than one hundred and twenty-five canvases. Velázquez was rewarded in 1658, when Philip honoured him with a knighthood.

The Maids of Honour draws us into Velázquez's life at the Alcazar Palace. The Infanta Margarita is restless. Two young maids of honour, Maria and Isabel, try to quieten her. The dwarf Maribárbola (one of Margarita's play-mates) stares out at us, and Nicolás, another dwarf, treads on the napping hound.

Velázquez portrayed himself as a proud and accomplished man wearing the red cross of Santiago, the emblem of knighthood.

17

When we look closely at this painting, we notice two more people. The king and queen are reflected in a mirror at the end of the dark room. Will they be part of Velázquez's painting, whose surface is hidden from view, or are they just visiting their daughter?

Velázquez created the illusion of great space by painting many different kinds of light. Sunshine pours in through a tall window at the right, flooding the foreground. A shadow area with dimly-lit figures in the middle of the picture is followed by another tall window spilling in just enough light to reveal the mirror reflecting the king and queen's image. A door in the back wall opens to another brightly-lit room. To make the lights stand out, Velázquez chose a greenish grey for the background.

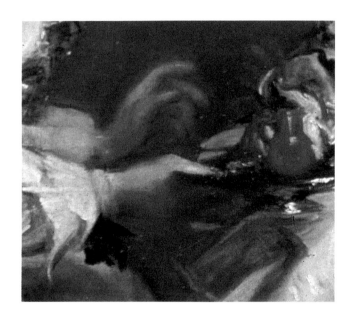

This detail shows the technique Velázquez used to create the appearance of movement.

Movement

Velázquez modelled the faces of the Infanta and her maids with delicacy. But he painted their hands blurred as though they were moving about. Velázquez painted bold blotches of black, red and white over the silver of Margarita's gown. On top of these blocks of colour, he used fine brush strokes to indicate the ribbon and lace.

Even though *The Maids of Honour* looks so real that we feel we could join the group, Velázquez has also created an air of mystery. In this picture of great riches, he painted the king and queen as ghostly images in a distant mirror. We sense their presence, but we also sense their faded glory.

18

19

THE BRIDGES FAMILY, 1804
John Constable, English (1776–1837), oil on canvas, 134 x 181 cm

John Constable was born in the first year of the **American Revolution** and lived at a time of global expansion, when personal success was prized. But Constable preferred the English countryside of his childhood to big cities and foreign travel. He wanted to express the beauty of the natural world by painting landscapes, but like other artists, he painted portraits to survive.

Outside light

George Bridges was a successful merchant who commissioned Constable to paint a family portrait. Constable took the assignment and did something completely unexpected. He brought the warm feeling of the landscape through an open window into the room. Constable recreated the transparent flickering light from the sky on the dresses of Mrs Bridges and her daughters; the glowing colours of the sunset brighten their faces. The dark clothing of Mr Bridges and his sons echoes the colour of the distant trees. Instead of creating a room filled with decorations, Constable painted what was important to him—the changing, natural light.

Constable painted *The Bridges Family* with the same kind of bold brushwork that he used in his landscape paintings. It seemed very simple compared to the polished portraits that were popular at the time.

Thomas Gainsborough, another celebrated English painter, lived half a century before Constable. In his drawing of a family group, he created the effect of soft light through the use of black and white chalk on rough-textured paper.

THE BELLELLI FAMILY, 1858–67
Edgar Degas, French (1834–1917), oil on canvas, 197 x 246 cm

*E*dgar Degas created an unusual group portrait when he painted his favourite aunt, Laura Bellelli, her husband Baron Gennaro Bellelli and their children. Looking at this painting, we can feel a great sadness. The family was in the process of a divorce.

The baroness is dressed entirely in black. She stands protectively over her daughter Giovanna, who looks unhappily out at the viewer. In the centre, Giulia sits with one foot tucked up, but with her arms in an impatient pose, her face the younger image of her mother's. With his back to the viewer, the baron looks away from his reading, but not at his family. All four seem to be remote from each other.

Tension

Degas increased the tense feeling in this scene with the colours and patterns he used. The children's crisp white pinafores make the large areas of black in the painting seem even darker. Patterns in the carpet and wallpaper give a feeling of comfort in contrast to the family discomfort.

Edgar Degas was twenty-four years old when he began painting and was trying to gain public recognition with a picture so large it would be noticed. Instead of creating a painting of nations at war—a popular theme with artists at the time—he showed the private drama of a troubled family.

In this detail, we can see the strength of Laura Bellelli's protective hand and the softness of her daughter's young hands.

LUNCHEON ON THE GRASS, 1866
Claude Monet, French (1840–1926), oil on canvas, 244 x 240 cm

Claude Monet was amazed by the magical way that the sunlight and shadows could change the appearance of colours. In 1865, he spent the summer painting in a forest to see and feel the colour of natural light. Monet's future wife Camille Doncieux and his good friend Frédéric Bazille were his models. Working outdoors, Monet painted small studies, which he later used to create this painting of life-size figures at a leisurely picnic.

Technical problems

Monet solved a technical problem and developed a new painting method in this early work. Ready-made paints, in tubes, had been available since 1841. They made working outside easier, but the linseed oil in the paint turned light colours yellow. Monet soaked out the unwanted oil with blotting paper, then added poppy seed oil and lead white paint, which did not turn yellow.

Using large brushes, Monet painted slabs of bright, opaque colours and created the sensation of being outside. He painted light blue highlights—the colours of the sky—on Bazille's suit. Monet lit up a plate of fruit with pale yellow brush strokes and painted lavender shadows on the white tablecloth to recreate the cool feeling of the forest.

In a close-up detail, we can see the bold yellow and blue highlights, which blend together when seen from far away.

FAMILY REUNION, 1865–69
Jean-Frédéric Bazille, French (1841–70), oil on canvas, 150 x 229 cm

Jean-Frédéric Bazille came from a prosperous family of wine growers and studied medicine to please his mother and father. Bazille was also a talented painter who spent much of his time with his friends Edouard Manet, Edgar Degas, Pierre-Auguste Renoir and Claude Monet, with whom he shared a studio. When Bazille failed medical school in 1864, his family supported his desire to paint.

A formal portrait

The year after Bazille had posed for Monet's painting *Luncheon on the Grass*, he used the same subject as Monet—stylish people in an outdoor setting—to create a formal portrait of his beloved family.

Bazille focused on the people, not the landscape, and created a dramatic scene. Bazille's relatives seem suspended in time, as though interrupted in conversation. Bazille is also there, looking out from behind his uncle, on the left.

Family Reunion, 1865-69

A theatrical setting

The trees and distant hills seem as flat as scenery in a play; the light on his cousin Thèrese, turning in her chair, resembles artificial, theatrical lighting; the hat and bouquet of flowers are like props at the front of a stage.

In 1868, Frédéric Bazille's talent was acknowledged when *Family Reunion* was selected for an important **exhibition** in Paris. But his painting career was cut short when a year later he was killed on the battlefield during the Franco-Prussian war.

THE MONET FAMILY IN THEIR GARDEN, 1874
Edouard Manet, French (1832–83), oil on canvas, 60 x 99 cm

'Every time I paint, I throw myself into the water in order to learn how to swim,' said Edouard Manet. He believed that there was not one 'right' way to paint but many. So Manet reinvented the art of painting every time he faced a canvas. In 1874, he painted outside for the first time with Claude Monet and Pierre-Auguste Renoir. Manet created this picture in appreciation of their friendship.

Lots of colour from a few paints

Manet's painting of the Monet family seems to sparkle with many colours. A close look shows that Manet actually achieved this effect by using very few colours. Madame Monet's dress is a block of pale pink with overlays of grey and a darker pink to suggest details. Manet used the same shade of pink in the sky beyond the trees. Both Monet's shirt and his son Jean's clothes are the same blue, but Manet added transparent patches of white over the boy's suit to indicate touches of sunlight. He created shadows by adding blue to the green of the grass and trees and splashed red shapes for the flowers along three sides of the garden.

Manet painted the same red on Jean's hat, in Madame Monet's fan and on the cockerel's comb to focus attention on the Monet family—and on the family of curious chickens!

*Pierre-Auguste Renoir often used his family and friends as models. Renoir drew his friend Edouard Manet's niece, Julie, using black **crayon** on rough-textured paper.*

MADAME CHARPENTIER AND HER CHILDREN GEORGETTE AND PAUL, 1878

Pierre-Auguste Renoir, French (1841–1919), oil on canvas, 151 x 187 cm

This portrait was Renoir's first important commission, and he gave Madame Charpentier all that she could wish for in a painting. Her husband was the publisher of books by France's greatest authors, including Emile Zola and Gustave Flaubert. Georges Charpentier spoiled his family with the luxuries of life. Renoir captured the splendid antiques, golden scrolls and beautiful crystal in Madame Charpentier's Japanese-style parlour. In this extravagant setting, the mother, her daughter Georgette, young son Paul, and even the dog, look comfortable.

Renoir captured the gestures and expressions of a close, happy family when he painted a portrait of his wife and children.

An eye for detail

Renoir had a sure eye for detail and a talent for painting skin tones. The room is busy with patterns and shapes, but Renoir painted a large, pale yellow carpet that draws our eyes towards the family. By repeating the red, blue and greenish gold of the walls in most of the furnishings, Renoir unified the background and made the figures stand out.

In nineteenth-century Paris, the only way for an artist to be successful was to have his work accepted in official exhibitions, which were known as 'Salons'. Renoir's family portrait was accepted by the Salon in April 1879. Madame Charpentier used her influence to ensure that the painting she so admired was prominently displayed, and Renoir's talent was publicly recognized for the first time.

PAUL HELLEU SKETCHING WITH HIS WIFE, 1889
John Singer Sargent, American (1856–1925), oil on canvas, 65 x 80 cm

*J*ohn Singer Sargent studied art in Paris when Edouard Manet, Pierre-Auguste Renoir and Claude Monet were at the centre of the art world. In 1887 he visited Monet at his country home. Sargent saw the master at work and admired Monet's visionary use of colour. The following year, Sargent created this intimate portrait of his best friend from art school, Paul Helleu, with his bride, Alice Louise.

Seasonal colours

We can almost feel the misty atmosphere of a cool autumn day in this painting. Sargent balanced his colours and his brush strokes to create this effect. He painted the new family in neutral colours—grey, tan and brown—with even strokes of the brush. He made the grass seem to shiver—dancing streaks of green paint shot with yellow and orange. Where the grass meets the water, it picks up cool, soft violet shadows.

Balance of colour

In this picture, Sargent used all of the colours of the rainbow: red, orange and yellow; blue, green and violet. He balanced the bright red colour of the canoe with the dull colours in the figures, the sharp green and yellow of the grass with the violet and blue of the shadows. This gives the painting an even tone.

This detail shows that Sargent warmed the grey colour of Alice Louise Helleu's blouse by mixing in the same red that he used for her lips—and for the canoe.

THE SCHUFFENECKER FAMILY, 1889
Paul Gauguin, French (1848–1903), oil on canvas, 72 x 90 cm

Paul Gauguin saw life through his dreams and his memories. Observing an event and sensing its emotional content, Gauguin looked for the most extreme lines, forms and colours to show his feelings. In his studio, he recalled these images and created a powerful expression of moments suspended in time.

The artist Emile Schuffenecker was Gauguin's closest friend for seventeen years. Often, when Gauguin could not pay his rent, he lived with the Schuffeneckers, who argued about his unpleasant manner.

Harsh reality

In this painting, Gauguin used extreme colours and shapes to create a disturbing atmosphere. A steep angle divides the room into two separate areas. The sharply-drawn lines describe the tension between the adults.

Emile occupies the blue zone, while Madame Schuffenecker sits in the yellow zone with the unhappy children. Emile steps forwards, as though to talk to his wife, but an easel blocks his way and shuts him into a corner.

Gauguin heightened the feeling of isolation in this painting by using strong, **primary colours**—red, yellow, and blue. The only softness is in the trees behind the bar-like window supports.

Mary Cassatt, an American painter who lived in Paris, was captivated by the love between mothers and their children. She often exhibited her paintings with Gauguin, Monet and Renoir.

THE FAMILY OF ACROBATS WITH APE, 1905
Pablo Picasso, Spanish (1881–1973), **gouache**, water-colour and **ink** on cardboard, 102 x 74 cm

The man who revolutionized modern art had his first success after he moved to Paris in 1904. Pablo Picasso was twenty-three years old and the leader of a group of painters and poets who struggled to make money and produce works of art. At night, they met in a local cafe to discuss their work and talk about life. When there was extra money, they often went to the theatre.

Picasso's favourite entertainment was the circus, with its bareback riders, tumblers and clowns. He sympathized with the poorly paid performers, whose offstage life was shabby compared to the glittering circus.

A private, gentle world

In this portrait, Picasso encloses a young circus family in a private world far away from the gaiety and noise of the ring. The range of rosy earth colours is as warm as this tender moment stolen between acts. Pale light and soft shadows enhance the intimate atmosphere. Even the ape, with its almost human expression, seeks to reflect the closeness of circus life.

The parent's hands catch our eye. They are strong and wiry—strong enough to catch a flying acrobat, but soft enough to caress a baby. Picasso may have identified himself—an artist who works magic in his paintings—with these performers who defy gravity in the circus ring.

Picasso expressed the young mother's complete devotion to her infant in this painting. The contrast between the dark clothing and the pale figures show how the mother's body shelters the baby.

PIANIST AND DRAUGHTS PLAYERS, 1924
Henri Matisse, French (1869–1954), oil on canvas, 72 x 91 cm

H enri Matisse was depressed by the misery caused by the First World War. In Paris, food was scarce, winters were cold and Matisse was exhausted by the difficulties of post-war life. In 1918 he left for Nice, in the south of France. There he found perfumed gardens—and a clear, silver light that inspired him.

The pleasure of painting and working with glorious colours made Matisse feel good. He captured his feeling of well-being in this painting of his richly-decorated living room, where his daughter Marguerite plays the piano, while his sons Pierre and Jean enjoy a game of draughts.

Angled picture
Matisse tilted the floor at a steep angle to spill the room out towards the viewer. Every inch is covered with design—flowers, rhythmic lines and images of Matisse's paintings. He painted pattern on top of pattern. The black and white of the draughts' board is repeated as stripes in the boys' shirts, on the tablecloth and on the edge of the carpet. The piano, a tall wardrobe and a sideboard—plain by comparison—define the sides of the room.

Matisse filled this painting with many shades of red—his **symbolic** colour for light. And he also shows the real light of Nice by painting a silvery colour on the back wall. A shadow cast by the sculpture tells us that there is a window to the right, beyond the edge of the picture.

Matisse loved music and played the violin himself. He often painted his children while they practised.

HOMMAGE A LOUIS DAVID, 1948–49
Fernand Léger, French (1881–1955), oil on canvas, 151 x 182 cm

During the Second World War, Fernand Léger went to the United States and discovered an exciting new world in New York. He found a city transformed by machinery. Strong men operated powerful equipment to build skyscrapers, bridges and undergrounds. Flashing neon signs lit the night in **garish** colours. Athletic women dressed in brightly-coloured shorts, like circus performers. To him, it was a completely unnatural world.

Mechanical forms

Back in France, Léger drew on these vivid images and his love of mechanical forms to create this painting of a family outing. The bicycles are like tubes; the men's arms and the fence like pipes. The tubular tree on the left becomes a bicycle lock. Black shadows on the ground seem like **sheet-metal** cut-outs. Even the leaves of the plants and the thick black outlines of the figures have a man-made quality.

The women wear the kind of clothing Léger had seen in America: boldly-patterned shorts in piercing colours, with belts like metal bands. In contrast, the men seem oddly overdressed. The people overlap each other, and there seems to be no real space around them. Doves perched on little clouds seem to be pasted on to the artificial-looking sky.

In his lifetime, Léger saw the world completely transformed by wars and by industrial progress. In this painting, he celebrated the positive effects of the machine age.

In this drawing of a mother and her son, Léger contrasted the soft pencil shading in the figures with the sharp edges of the window.

SIX STUDIES FOR FAMILY GROUP, 1948
Henry Moore, English (1898–1986), pencil with wax crayon, water-colour and ink, 51 x 38 cm

Henry Moore's father was a coal miner. He spent long, gruelling hours in the mines carving coal from the rocks, while his wife Mary struggled to care for their eight children. Like his father, Henry Moore also carved—but he became a sculptor who **extracted** his vision of life from great blocks of stone, often using the family group as his subject.

Sculpture

Creating sculpture is exhausting and time-consuming work. Every few months, Moore would put down his chisels to paint and draw. He said that drawing was a way to keep mentally fit—to feed his imagination and to develop ideas for new projects. In this drawing, Moore divided his paper into six areas and studied different possibilities for a sculpture. The simplified figures echo the forms of the **primitive sculpture** he admired.

Moore began with wax crayons, then painted in water-colour. Using coloured inks, he drew curved lines on the arms, legs and heads. As he drew these 'section lines', Moore mentally carved the figures of the parents into large sheltering forms. Highlights and dark tones create the effect of light and shadow. Moore was so practised at drawing that he was able to draw rapidly and shape powerful images. But he believed that if he made highly finished drawings, his sculpture would suffer and look dull and lifeless.

A devoted husband and father, Moore returned to the family group again and again in drawing and in sculpture.

Henry Moore created blocks of colour with large crayons to shape the child's figure and the parents' tender hands.

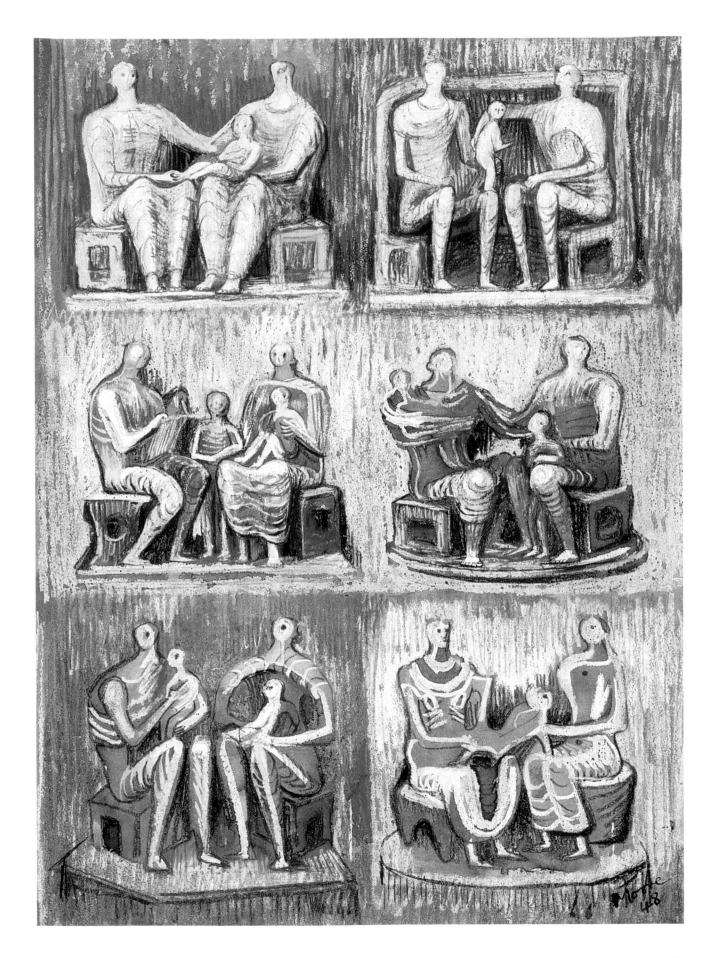

HAITIAN FAMILY, 1962
Castera Bazile, Haitian (1923–65), oil on **Masonite**, 60 x 40 cm

Haiti is part of an island in the West Indies. In 1791 a black slave called Toussaint-L'Ouverture led a revolt against the French who had colonized the island. This led to the formation of the first black republic in the world in 1804.

Castera Bazile realized his dream to be an artist in the capital city, Port-au-Prince. He developed his talent at the art centre, where truck drivers, lawyers and farmers painted together and exhibited their work. Bazile found inspiration in his African **heritage**, in Haitian folklore and in everyday life.

The despair of poverty

In this family group, Bazile portrays the mother as an imposing figure, gently nursing her baby. Her husband holds his head in despair. The other child, deprived of the joys of youth, seems strangely old. The parents are too poor to buy shoes or clothes for the children.

The stillness of the mother's figure creates a visual contrast with angles and shapes that lead our eyes across the painting—angles in the father's arms, in the blank wall and in the soaring trunk of the tree.

Bazile used images and jewel-like colours that have meaning in the Haitian **voodoo religion**. The child's red-and-white shirt is believed to protect against evil magic. Red and blue in the mother's clothes stand for warmth and strength. And the tree symbolizes a passageway to the spirit world, which offers the only relief from grinding poverty.

Jacques-Richard Chery, an artist who also worked at the Port-au-Prince Art Centre, painted bold shapes and sharp angles in Mother and Child.

44

45

Glossary and Index

AMERICAN REVOLUTION: the civil war between 1775 and 1783 which led to the independence of the United States from Britain.

APPRENTICE: a person who works for a master artist in exchange for training. In the seventeenth century, an apprentice's tasks included preparing paints, mounting canvases on to frames and cleaning up the painting studio. After a long period of training, talented apprentices could become independent artists if they exhibited their works and captured the attention of **patrons**.

CANVAS: a woven fabric (often linen or cotton) used as a painting surface. It is usually stretched tight and stapled on to a wooden frame in order to produce a flat, unwrinkled surface.

CARTOON: a full-sized, detailed drawing on heavy paper that the artist transfers on to the painting surface as a guide. The term is derived from the Italian name for the paper, *cartone*.

COMMISSION: (1) a work of art produced at the request of a wealthy patron. (2) The appointment of an artist to create such a work of art.

CRAYON: a coloured pencil that can be made of wax or chalk.

DESIGN: (1) the arrangement of objects and figures in a painting through the combination of colours and shapes. This is also called composition. (2) A pattern of shapes on a surface.

ENAMEL: (1) a **glaze** made of powdered coloured glass, applied to metal and backed, or fired, at a high temperature to produce a shiny surface. (2) A paint that has a shiny, smooth surface when it dries.

EXHIBITION: a display of paintings by one artist or several for people to view.

EXTRACT: to draw out from or to pull out.

FRESCO: a method of painting on to wet plaster, usually with water-colour, to create a picture in which the paint is absorbed into the wall instead of remaining on the surface.

GARISH: bright and bold, almost showy.

GLAZE: a **transparent**, or almost transparent, thinned-down layer of paint applied over dry paint, allowing the colours underneath to show through.

GOUACHE: an **opaque** form of water-colour, which is also called tempera or body-colour.

HERITAGE: anything passed down from ancestors or past ages.

HOLY ROMAN EMPEROR: an inherited title for rulers who governed their own lands and held certain powers over the rest of the empire which consisted mainly of modern-day Germany and Austria.

INK: usually, a jet-black fluid made of powdered carbon mixed with water. Ink drawings can be made with dark lines and diluted tones of grey. Inks are also made in colours and used in paintings.

MASONITE: a kind of dark brown hardboard.

OIL PAINT: pigment is combined with oil (usually linseed or poppy oil). Oil paint is never mixed with water. It is washed off brushes with turpentine. Oil paint dries slowly, which enables artists to work on a painting for a long time.

OPAQUE: not letting light pass through. Opaque paints hide what is under them. (The opposite of **transparent**.)

PATRON: one who supports the arts or an individual artist.

PRIMARY COLOURS: those colours from which all others can be made. They are red, yellow and blue.

PRIMITIVE SCULPTURE: a style of sculpture which can look untrained. A lot of primitive sculpture comes from Africa.

PROFILE: the side-on view of a person.

SHEET-METAL: metal that has been beaten into a very fine, flat sheet.

SYMBOLIC: something which has another meaning; a sign.

TRADEMARK: a distinctive and special sign or symbol which belongs to a particular person.

TRANSPARENT: allowing light to pass through so colours underneath can be seen. (The opposite to **opaque**.)

TROMPE L'OEIL: a technique used to paint a scene so realistically that the viewer may be tricked into thinking that people and objects in the picture are real—that the flat surface of the painting is an actual space. In sixteenth and seventeenth-century Italian art, this technique was often used to create the illusion of soaring domes and arches in rooms with flat ceilings.

WATER-COLOUR: pigment is combined with a water-based substance. Water-colour paint is thinned with water, and areas of paper are often left uncovered to produce highlights. Water-colour paint was first used 37,000 years ago by cave dwellers who created the first wall paintings.

VOODOO RELIGION: superstitious beliefs and practices of African origin, which used to involve serpent worship, human sacrifice and cannibalism.

Credits